PIANO
Prep
Test

This book belongs to:

....

Date of Prep Test:

....

Examiner's signature:

....

The Associated Board of the Royal Schools of Music

PIANO PREP TEST

Dear piano player

The first step on a journey is always exciting. Some preparation before you begin is always a good plan and makes the journey much smoother and easier. Your Prep Test will make sure you have all you need as you start your own musical journey and your teacher will guide you safely towards the sort of good playing that will last a lifetime.

The Prep Test is designed to be taken when you have been playing for a few terms. Built into it are all the sorts of skills you will be developing at this stage, such as a sense of pitch and rhythm, controlled and even playing, accuracy and quality of sound or 'tone'. The test takes around 10 minutes to cover the tunes, pieces and listening games. You will be playing to a very experienced musician who will be interested to hear all that you do well and will also make suggestions to help you with your future playing. The examiner will write all his or her comments on your certificate, which will be given to you at the end of the test.

This book contains everything you need to do the Prep Test, explaining how each part will help to develop your musical skills and giving advice on what the examiner will be looking for. For the set piece, you can choose to play either one of the two pieces printed on pages 4 and 5 of this book, or a piece from one of the *Party Time!* for Piano volumes or *Roundabout* (all published by the Board). Your 'own choice' piece is just that; so pick something you really enjoy playing.

We hope you enjoy the tunes, pieces and musical games, as well as the illustrations and Fun Page. We hope also that this is the first step of what will be an exciting and life-long musical journey.

Now on to the music!

Clara Taylor.

Chief Examiner

1 Tunes

The examiner will want to hear you play all three of these tunes. You will have to play them from memory, so once you have learnt them don't forget to keep your book closed when you are practising!

a) Walking

Try to play this tune as evenly and smoothly as possible.
The musical term for this sort of playing is 'legato'.

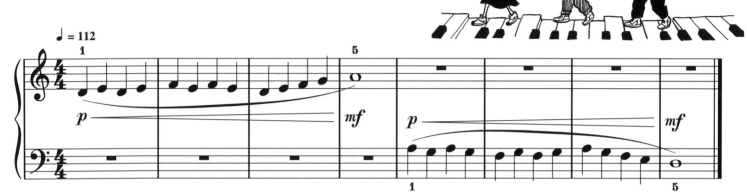

b) Rocking

The name of this tune tells you how it should be played: rock from finger to finger, lifting them cleanly off the keys.

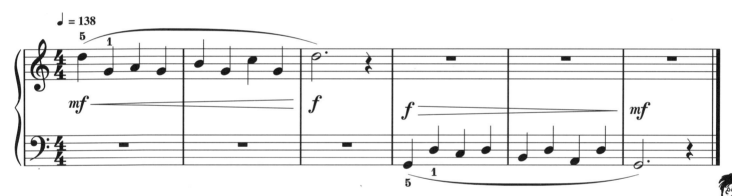

c) Hopping

You will need a good hand shape to play the two-part chords in this tune, so keep your fingers curved and your wrists level – imagine you are holding a small ball under each hand. The dots under and over some of the chords mean that these should be detached (musicians say 'staccato'), so remember to jump neatly off the keys.

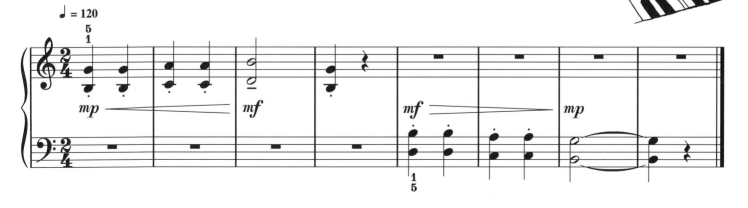

☀ Alan Bullard featured alot in piano time

2 Set Piece

Your set piece can be either one of the pieces printed on these two pages — 'Boating Lake' or 'Jogalong!' — or any piece from Alan Haughton's *Roundabout* or from one of the *Party Time!* for Piano volumes (all published by the Board). Your teacher will help you to choose the right piece.

3 Own Choice Piece

This is the second piece that you play and, because we want it to be something you really enjoy, we have left the choice of piece up to you. This means that you are free to choose any piece at all, even one of the set pieces (as long as it is different from your first piece!).

Don't forget to show your 'own choice' piece to the examiner, as he or she will want to know what you are going to play.

Boating Lake

Alan Bullard

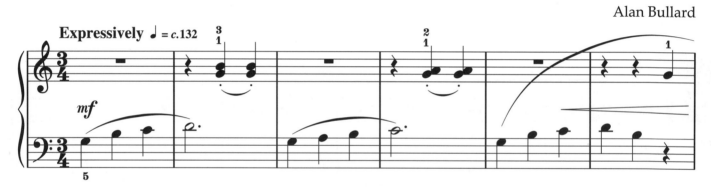

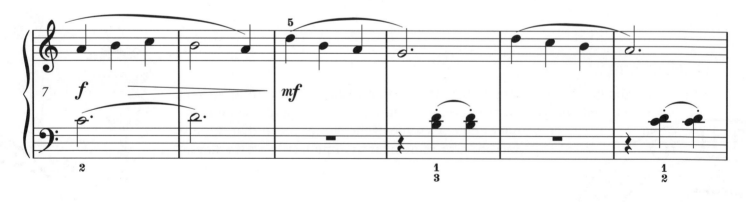

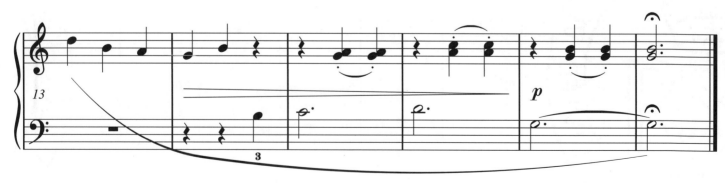

Jogalong!

Alan Bullard

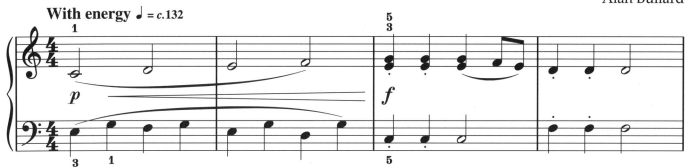

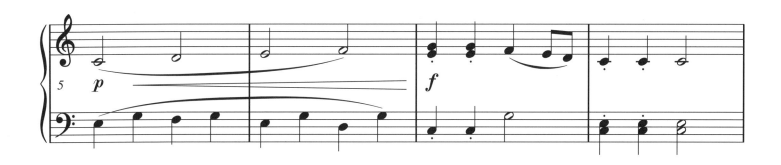

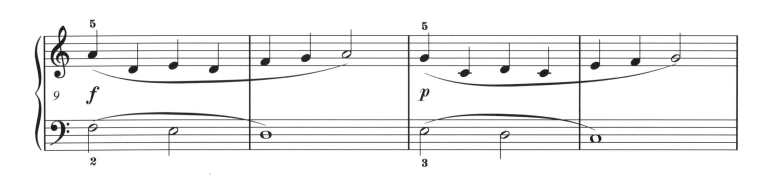

✳ *Introduction to aural tests*

4 Listening Games

In these Games the examiner will be playing pieces of music like the examples printed below.

Game A: Clapping the beat

In this first game, the examiner will play a short piece in 2 or 3 time. You should join in as soon as possible by clapping or tapping the beat.

All music has a beat, so you can practise this game at home with your friends whenever you are listening to music on the radio or a recording. You can clap along to pop music too!

Game B: Echoes

In this game, the examiner will clap two simple rhythms in 2 or 3 time. After each one, you should clap the rhythm back to the examiner in time and as an echo. The examiner will count in two bars.

Practise this game at home with a friend or parent. Did you clap *exactly* the same rhythm? Did you clap it back straightaway or was there a pause?

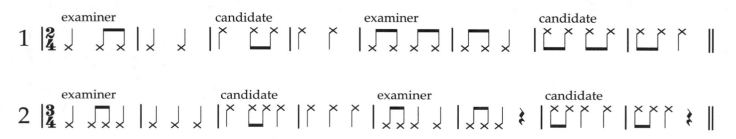

Game C: Finding the notes

Now the examiner will play a group of three notes to you, two times through. The game is to sing these notes back to the examiner after the second playing — if you don't want to sing, you can play the notes on the piano (in this case, the examiner will tell you the name of the starting note). The notes will be within a range of a third and will be white notes only. They will be played in 'free time' too, so you don't need to worry about the rhythm.

Game D: What can you hear?

In this last game, listen as the examiner plays another short piece of music. The examiner will want to know whether the piece was played loudly or quietly (the 'dynamic' of the piece), or whether it was fast or slow (the 'tempo' of the piece). The examiner will chose one of these and tell you which one to listen out for before he or she plays.

Practise this game at home with your friends whenever you are playing or listening to a piece of music.

i) Is this piece loud or quiet?

ii) Is this piece fast or slow?

Fun Page

Music is written down on five lines known as a 'stave'. A few empty staves are printed below: you can use these to practise drawing notes, rests, clefs and time signatures (if you don't understand any of these words, ask your teacher or look in *First Steps in Music Theory* published by the Associated Board). Or you can write down some tunes of your own.

Word Search

This word search contains 12 musical words, listed below, which have been mentioned elsewhere in the book. How many can you find? Do you know what they all mean?

Words to find:
legato
staccato
beat
dynamic
tempo
stave
chord
piano
rhythm
bar
note
rest

D	C	N	O	T	E	W	B	A	R
A	Y	E	R	U	P	K	E	C	H
L	F	N	G	R	I	O	A	R	Y
U	S	T	A	C	C	A	T	O	T
W	T	E	P	M	H	I	W	P	H
J	A	Z	P	Y	I	T	A	M	M
O	V	T	I	X	H	C	L	E	B
L	E	G	A	T	O	F	N	T	U
D	K	Y	N	U	Q	R	E	S	T
A	C	H	O	R	D	U	L	Y	B

We hope you enjoyed doing the Prep Test and look forward to seeing you at Grade 1!